EXPLORE MANC

Ultimate Travel Guide to Discovering The the Vibrant City

Steve Kaswui

Rights Reserved.

rights reserved. Except for brief quotations used in critical reviews and other non-commercial uses permitted by copyright law, no part of this publication may be copied, distributed, or transmitted in any way without the publisher's prior written consent, including by photocopying, recording, or other electronic or mechanical methods. If you want to ask for permission, write to the publisher.
copyright © Steve Kaswui

TABLE OF CONTENTS

Welcome to Manchester
CHAPTER 1: INTRODUCTION
Manchester's Brief History
Manchester's Weather
Best Time to Visit Manchester
How To Get There
Top 15 Reasons To Plan A Trip To Manchester As Your Next Vacation Destination
CHAPTER 2: TIPS AND CONSIDERATIONS
Visiting Manchester On A Budget
Getting Around Manchester
Shopping In Manchester
5 Inexpensive Manchester Hotel Option
5 Luxurious Places To Stay In Manchester
CHAPTER 3
Top 5 Event In Manchester
3 Days Manchester Travel Plan
7 Days Manchester Travel Plan
CHAPTER 4: PLANNING A TRIP TO MANCHESTER
What To Take For Your Trip
Night Spot In Manchester
Culture And People
CHAPTER 5
Top 10 Best Local Cuisine In Manchester
Money Matters And Saving Tips

Local Customs And Etiquette

Tipping In Manchester

CHAPTER 6: TIPS AND CONSIDERATION ENTRY REQUIREMENT

Safety And Preparedness

What To Do And What To Avoid When Visiting manchester

CHAPTER 7: UNDERSTANDING INTERNATIONAL TRANSACTION FEES

Avoid Cell Phone Roaming Charges

Consider A Manchester Sim Card Or Mifi Device

Download Offline Map

Learn Basic Language

Cash At The Airport Is Expensive

CONCLUSION

Additional Resources And Contact Information

Welcome to Manchester

Emma had always dreamt of visiting Manchester, the vibrant city known for its rich history, iconic music scene, and famous football clubs. Finally, her long-awaited trip became a reality. With her suitcase packed and excitement bubbling within her, Emma embarked on a journey that would leave an indelible mark on her heart.

As Emma stepped off the train at Manchester Piccadilly station, she couldn't help but marvel at the architectural beauty that surrounded her. The mix of old and modern buildings told tales of a city that had grown and evolved over the years. With a map in hand, she navigated through the bustling streets, eager to explore every nook and cranny of this remarkable place.

Her first stop was the Manchester Museum, a treasure trove of art, culture, and history. As she strolled through the exhibits, Emma was captivated by the artifacts from different civilizations and eras. From Egyptian mummies to dinosaur skeletons, each display held a story waiting to be discovered. She found herself immersed in the wonders of the world, feeling as though she had traveled through time and space.

The next day, Emma ventured into the vibrant Northern Quarter, a hub of creativity and independent businesses. The streets were adorned with colorful street art, and the aroma of freshly brewed coffee wafted through the air. She wandered into quirky vintage stores, where she found unique clothing and accessories that spoke to her eclectic taste. With her newfound treasures in hand, she settled into a cozy café, sipping her coffee and relishing the lively atmosphere around her.

No visit to Manchester would be complete without indulging in its musical heritage. Emma secured tickets to a live performance at the legendary Manchester Arena. The electrifying energy of the crowd as the band took the stage was infectious. The music reverberated through her veins, as she danced and sang along with thousands of other fans. In that moment, she felt a deep connection with the city and understood why Manchester was renowned for its iconic music scene.

Emma's journey also took her to Old Trafford, the iconic home of Manchester United. As a football enthusiast, she couldn't contain her excitement as she entered the stadium. The history and legacy of the club were palpable, and she stood in awe, imagining the roar of the crowd during intense matches. She took a guided tour of the stadium, walking through the players' tunnel and sitting in the stands, soaking in the atmosphere of a place that had witnessed countless historic moments.

On her final day, Emma decided to explore Manchester's natural beauty. She visited Heaton Park, a sprawling green oasis nestled within the city. The park's serene lakes, blooming gardens, and vast open spaces provided a tranquil escape from the urban hustle. Emma took a leisurely stroll, breathing in the fresh air and reflecting on the unforgettable experiences she had had in Manchester.

As Emma bid farewell to the city, she carried with her cherished memories and a newfound love for Manchester. The vibrant culture, friendly people, and the city's ability to seamlessly blend its rich history with modernity had left an indelible mark on her. She promised herself that she would return one day, eager to uncover more of Manchester's hidden gems and create new adventures in this extraordinary place.

CHAPTER 1: INTRODUCTION

Manchester's Brief History

Manchester, located in the northwest of England, has a rich and fascinating history that spans centuries. Originally a small Roman settlement known as "Mancunium," the city evolved into a significant industrial powerhouse during the Industrial Revolution.

In the 18th century, Manchester became a center for textile production, particularly cotton. The construction of canals and the development of steam-powered machinery revolutionized the textile industry, leading to the rapid growth of Manchester's mills and factories. The city's population exploded as workers flocked to the area in search of employment, transforming Manchester into a bustling metropolis.

Manchester's industrial prosperity continued into the 19th century, earning it the title of "Cottonopolis" due to its dominance in cotton production. The city's factories and warehouses were a hub of activity, and Manchester's cotton goods were exported worldwide, solidifying its position as a global trading center.

During this period, Manchester played a pivotal role in the fight for workers' rights and social reform. The Peterloo Massacre of 1819, in which peaceful protesters demanding political representation were brutally suppressed, brought attention to the need for democratic reform and sparked a wave of activism.

As the 20th century dawned, Manchester faced significant challenges. The decline of the textile industry, economic hardships, and the impact of World War II took a toll on the city. However, Manchester displayed remarkable resilience, adapting to new industries and reinventing itself as a hub of innovation and culture.

In recent decades, Manchester has experienced a renaissance. It has become a vibrant and cosmopolitan city, known for its thriving music scene, world-class universities, and sporting prowess. The redevelopment of the city center and the construction of iconic structures such as the revitalized Manchester Central Library and the distinctive Beetham Tower have contributed to its modern skyline.

Manchester's sporting heritage is also a point of pride for its residents. The city is home to two world-renowned football clubs, Manchester United and Manchester City, and has hosted major sporting events such as the 2002 Commonwealth Games and matches during the 2012 Olympics.

Today, Manchester is a thriving city that embraces its history while looking towards the future. Its blend of industrial heritage, cultural diversity, and vibrant energy make it an appealing destination for visitors from around the world. With ongoing development and regeneration projects, Manchester continues to evolve, showcasing its resilience and determination to remain a dynamic and influential city.

Manchester's Weather

Manchester's weather is renowned for being unpredictable and is frequently referred to as having "four seasons in one day." The city, which is found in the northwest of England, enjoys a temperate marine environment because of its closeness to the Irish Sea.

Manchester regularly experiences rain, and the city receives a sizable amount of precipitation all year long. Any time is likely to bring showers, which are frequently accompanied by cloudy skies. Manchester is renowned for its vivid greenery and lush green surroundings, both of which are a result of the city's humidity.

The average high temperature in the city is around 20°C (68°F) in the summer and 8°C (46°F) in the winter. It is important to remember that Manchester's weather may be unpredictable, so it is best to be ready for unforeseen shifts. In a single day, it is not unusual to have a mix of sunshine, rain, and even hail.

Manchester experiences relatively mild winters compared to other parts of the UK because of the Atlantic Ocean's influence on the city's weather patterns. In the winter, snowfall is uncommon but not unheard of. Manchester's summers are normally warm and enjoyable, with sporadic heatwaves occasionally raising temperatures above 25°C (77°F).

Manchester's inhabitants have learned to accept and adjust to the conditions despite the unpredictable weather. While the availability of parks and open areas provides for outdoor enjoyment when the weather is suitable, the city's thriving cultural scene offers a choice of indoor attractions and activities to enjoy on rainy days.

Best Time to Visit Manchester

The best time to visit Manchester largely depends on personal preferences and interests. However, there are a few factors to consider when planning your trip to this vibrant city.

Summer, from June to August, is a popular time to visit Manchester. The weather is generally mild, with average temperatures ranging from 15°C (59°F) to 20°C (68°F). This is an excellent time to explore the city's outdoor attractions, such as the beautiful parks and gardens, and enjoy outdoor events and festivals. The longer daylight hours also provide more time to explore the city.

Spring (March to May) and autumn (September to November) are also favorable seasons to visit Manchester. The weather during these months is generally pleasant, with milder temperatures and fewer crowds compared to the summer months. Spring brings blooming flowers and rejuvenated green spaces, while autumn showcases the city's beautiful foliage.

Winter, from December to February, can be cold and wet in Manchester. However, this time of year has its charm, especially during the festive season. Christmas markets, ice skating rinks, and cozy cafes offer a warm and inviting atmosphere. It is worth noting that winter is also the football season, so sports enthusiasts may want to plan their visit accordingly to catch a match at one of Manchester's renowned stadiums.

Ultimately, the best time to visit Manchester depends on personal preferences. Whether you enjoy the buzz of summer festivals, the beauty of spring blooms, the colors of autumn, or the festive cheer of winter, Manchester offers something for everyone year-round. Consider your interests and desired activities to choose the season that suits you best.

How To Get There

Manchester, located in the northwest of England, is a well-connected city with various transportation options for travelers. Here are some common ways to get to Manchester:

- **By Air:**
  Manchester Airport (MAN) is the primary international airport serving the city. It is well-connected to major cities around the world, offering direct flights from various destinations. From the airport, you can easily reach the city center by train, taxi, or bus. The airport has its own train station, Manchester Airport Station, with frequent services to Manchester Piccadilly, the city's main railway hub.
- **By Train:**
  Manchester has excellent railway connections, making it easily accessible from other parts of the UK. Major train

stations in Manchester include Manchester Piccadilly, Manchester Victoria, and Manchester Oxford Road. Direct train services operate from cities like London, Edinburgh, Birmingham, and Liverpool. High-speed trains, such as the Virgin Trains' West Coast Main Line, provide fast connections to Manchester.

- **By Bus:**

National Express and Megabus are two popular coach companies that offer services to Manchester from various cities across the UK. The buses arrive at Manchester Central Coach Station, which is located in the city center. From there, you can easily access other parts of Manchester using public transportation or taxis.

- **By Car:**

Manchester is well-connected to the national motorway network, with the M60 orbital motorway encircling the city. The M62, M56, M61, and M6 motorways also provide convenient access to Manchester. However, keep in mind that traffic congestion can be an issue, especially during peak hours. There are numerous car parks available in the city center for those who prefer to drive.

- **By Coach:**

If you are traveling from within the UK, coach services like National Express and Megabus offer affordable and convenient options to reach Manchester. These coaches operate from various cities and towns across the country, with frequent services to Manchester.

Once you arrive in Manchester, the city has an extensive public transportation network, including trams, buses, and trains, making it easy to get around and explore the different areas. Taxis and ride-hailing services are also readily available for convenient transportation within the city.

Plan your journey ahead of time, check the schedules and fares, and consider using public transportation options to avoid traffic congestion and parking hassles in the city center.

Top 15 Reasons To Plan A Trip To Manchester As Your Next Vacation Destination

1. **Rich History:** Manchester boasts a fascinating history, from its industrial heritage to its pivotal role in the fight for workers' rights and social reform.
2. **Vibrant Culture:** The city is a cultural hub, with numerous art galleries, museums, and theaters showcasing a diverse range of artistic expressions.
3. **Iconic Music Scene:** Manchester has a legendary music heritage, with famous bands like Oasis and The Smiths originating from the city. Experience live music in iconic venues and soak in the city's musical atmosphere.
4. **Football Fever:** Home to two world-renowned football clubs, Manchester United and Manchester City, the city is a paradise for football enthusiasts. Catch a match and witness the electrifying atmosphere at Old Trafford or the Etihad Stadium.
5. **Outstanding Architecture:** Manchester boasts a mix of architectural styles, from

historic buildings like the Manchester Town Hall to modern structures like the Beetham Tower, offering architectural delights for enthusiasts.
6. **Shopping Paradise:** Explore Manchester's vibrant shopping scene, from high-end fashion brands in the city center to unique boutiques in the Northern Quarter and vintage stores in Afflecks.
7. **Culinary Delights:** Manchester offers a diverse range of culinary experiences, with a thriving food and drink scene. Enjoy international cuisines, trendy cafes, and traditional British pubs.
8. **Festivals and Events:** The city hosts numerous festivals throughout the year, including the Manchester International Festival, Manchester Pride, and the Christmas markets, providing vibrant and exciting experiences.
9. **Beautiful Parks and Green Spaces:** Manchester is known for its abundance of parks and green spaces, such as Heaton Park and Fletcher Moss Botanical Garden, offering serene retreats amidst the urban hustle.
10. **World-class Universities**: Manchester is home to prestigious universities, including the University of Manchester and

Manchester Metropolitan University. Explore their campuses and soak in the vibrant student culture.

11. **Great Transportation Links:** With excellent transport connections, Manchester is easily accessible by air, train, and road, making it a convenient gateway for exploring other parts of the UK.
12. **Artistic Street Culture:** The streets of Manchester are adorned with vibrant street art, showcasing the city's creative spirit. Take a stroll through the Northern Quarter to discover stunning murals and graffiti.
13. **Industrial Heritage:** Learn about Manchester's industrial past by visiting sites like the Science and Industry Museum, which tells the story of the city's pioneering achievements.
14. **Surrounding Natural Beauty:** Manchester is surrounded by stunning landscapes, including the Peak District National Park, which offers opportunities for hiking, cycling, and exploring picturesque villages.
15. **Friendly and Welcoming Atmosphere:** Above all, the people of Manchester are known for their friendly and welcoming nature, making visitors feel at home and enhancing the overall experience of the city.

CHAPTER 2: TIPS AND CONSIDERATIONS

Visiting Manchester On A Budget

Visiting Manchester on a budget can be an exciting and rewarding experience. As a vibrant city in the northwest of England, Manchester offers a rich cultural heritage, impressive architecture, and a buzzing atmosphere. With a little planning and some smart choices, you can make the most of your trip without breaking the bank.

Firstly, when it comes to accommodation, consider staying in budget-friendly options such as hostels or budget hotels. Manchester has a range of affordable accommodations that offer comfortable stays at a fraction of the cost of luxury hotels. Look for deals and discounts online to further reduce your expenses.

Transportation in Manchester is also reasonably priced and convenient. The city has an extensive public transportation network, including buses and trams, which can take you to most attractions. Consider purchasing a day or week pass for unlimited travel, as this can save you money compared to individual tickets.

One of the highlights of visiting Manchester is its diverse cultural scene. Take advantage of the many free or low-cost attractions available. The city boasts numerous museums and galleries that offer free admission, such as the Manchester Museum, the Whitworth Art Gallery, and the National Football Museum. Explore the vibrant street art scene in the Northern Quarter, or take a stroll along the picturesque canals and green spaces like Castlefield and Heaton Park.

Food and dining can also be enjoyed on a budget in Manchester. The city is known for its diverse culinary offerings, including affordable street food markets and budget-friendly eateries. Explore the famous Curry Mile in Rusholme, where you can find delicious and inexpensive South Asian cuisine. Additionally, many pubs and bars offer lunchtime deals and happy hour specials, allowing you to enjoy a hearty meal or drinks without breaking the bank.

Lastly, don't miss out on Manchester's iconic music scene. Keep an eye out for free or low-cost gigs and concerts happening at venues like Night and Day Café, Band on the Wall, or Soup Kitchen. You can also visit music memorabilia stores or independent record shops to soak up the city's rich musical heritage.

Getting Around Manchester

1. **Train**

    Manchester has two main train stations: Piccadilly and Victoria. Trains can be a convenient way to get to Manchester from other parts of the UK, but they can also be expensive. A single adult train ticket from London to Manchester typically costs around £50.00.

2. **Airport:**

    Manchester Airport is located 10 miles south of the city center. The airport is served by a number of airlines, and flights are available to most major cities in the UK and Europe.

A single adult return flight from London to Manchester typically costs around £100.00.

Shopping In Manchester

Manchester is a great city for shopping. There are a wide variety of stores to choose from, and prices are generally very reasonable. Here are some of the best places to shop in Manchester, along with the average prices you can expect to pay:

1. **Department stores:** Manchester has a number of large department stores, such as Selfridges, Debenhams, and John Lewis. These stores offer a wide variety of merchandise, from clothes and shoes to homewares and electronics. Expect to pay around £20 for a pair of jeans, £30 for a t-shirt, and £50 for a pair of shoes.
2. **High street stores:** Manchester's high streets are home to a wide variety of independent stores, as well as chains such as Topshop, H&M, and Zara. These stores offer a great selection of clothes, shoes, and accessories. Expect to pay around £15 for a pair of jeans, £20 for a t-shirt, and £30 for a pair of shoes.
3. **Markets:** Manchester has a number of markets, where you can find everything from fresh produce to clothes and souvenirs. Some of the most popular markets include the Arndale Market, the Corn Exchange, and the Affleck's Palace Market. Expect to pay around £5 for a t-shirt, £10 for a pair of jeans, and £15 for a pair of shoes.
4. **Online shopping:** Manchester also has a thriving online shopping scene. You can find a wide variety of stores to choose from, and prices are often even lower than in physical stores. Expect to pay around £10 for a

T-shirt, £15 for a pair of jeans, and £20 for a pair of shoes. Some of the most popular online stores include Amazon, Asos, and Zalando.

5 Inexpensive Manchester Hotel Option

1. ibis budget Manchester Centre Pollard Street. This hotel is located in the city center and offers simple rooms with complimentary Wi-Fi, plus a 24-hour snack shop. Prices start from £30 per night.

2. Premier Inn Manchester City Centre - Arena. This hotel is also located in the city center and offers modern rooms with flat-screen TVs and free Wi-Fi. Prices start from £35 per night.

3. Travelodge Manchester Piccadilly. This hotel is located just a short walk from Piccadilly Gardens and offers comfortable rooms with flat-screen TVs and free Wi-Fi. Prices start from £30 per night.

4. easyHotel Manchester City Centre. This hotel is located in the city center and offers basic rooms with free Wi-Fi. Prices start from £25 per night.

5. The Leven. This hotel is located in the Northern Quarter and offers stylish rooms with free Wi-Fi. Prices start from £40 per night.

5 Luxurious Places To Stay In Manchester

1. Hotel Gotham. This art deco hotel is located in the heart of Manchester city centre and is within walking distance of many popular

attractions, such as the Manchester Arena, the National Football Museum, and the Bridgewater Hall. The hotel has a rooftop bar with stunning views of the city, a spa, and a gym. Rooms start at £200 per night.

2. The Lowry Hotel. This contemporary hotel is located on the banks of the River Irwell and has views of the city skyline. The hotel has a spa, a gym, and two restaurants. Rooms start at £250 per night.

3. The Edwardian Manchester, A Radisson Collection Hotel. This historic hotel is located in the Free Trade Hall, a Grade I listed building in Manchester city centre. The hotel has a spa, a gym, and a restaurant. Rooms start at £150 per night.

4. Hilton Manchester Deansgate. This modern hotel is located in the heart of Manchester city centre and is within walking distance of many popular attractions, such as the Manchester Arena, the National Football Museum, and the Bridgewater Hall. The hotel has a spa, a gym, and a restaurant. Rooms start at £100 per night.

5. Maldron Hotel Manchester City Centre. This 4-star hotel is located in Manchester city centre and is within walking distance of many popular attractions, such as the Manchester Arena, the National Football Museum, and the Bridgewater Hall. The hotel has a gym and a restaurant. Rooms start at £75 per night.

CHAPTER 3

Top 5 Event In Manchester

1. **Manchester International Festival (MIF):**
   The Manchester International Festival is a biennial event that showcases innovative and boundary-pushing art, music, theater, and dance performances. The festival attracts renowned artists from around the world, and its diverse program features a wide range of performances and installations. MIF takes place at various venues across the city, transforming Manchester into a hub of creativity and cultural exchange.

2. **Manchester Pride:**
   Manchester Pride is one of the UK's largest LGBTQ+ celebrations, held annually over a long weekend. The event features a colorful

and vibrant parade through the city center, followed by a series of performances, parties, and community events. Manchester Pride aims to promote equality and diversity while providing a platform for LGBTQ+ artists and performers. The festival creates a joyous and inclusive atmosphere, attracting visitors from all over the country.

3. **Parklife Festival:**

Parklife Festival is a two-day music festival held in Heaton Park, featuring an impressive lineup of renowned artists from the worlds of electronic, indie, and hip-hop music. With multiple stages and a lively atmosphere, Parklife attracts music enthusiasts from across the country. The festival offers a mix of established acts and emerging talents, providing a dynamic and energetic experience for attendees.

4. **Manchester Christmas Markets:**

    The Manchester Christmas Markets are a beloved annual event that signals the start of the festive season in the city. The markets consist of multiple wooden chalets selling a wide variety of crafts, gifts, and delicious food and drink. Visitors can wander through the festive stalls, enjoy live music, and savor traditional treats like mulled wine and roasted chestnuts. The markets create a magical atmosphere, making it a perfect place to get into the holiday spirit.

3 Days Manchester Travel Plan

Day 1:

Morning:

- Start your day by visiting the iconic Manchester Cathedral. Take a self-guided tour and admire the stunning architecture and beautiful stained glass windows. Admission is free, but donations are appreciated.
- Next, head to the nearby Chetham's Library, one of the oldest public libraries in the English-speaking world. Explore the historic reading rooms and browse through the collection of rare books and manuscripts. Admission is free.

Lunch:

- Grab a quick and affordable lunch at the Arndale Market, located in the heart of the city. The market offers a variety of food stalls, ranging from local delicacies to international cuisine.

Afternoon:

- Visit the Manchester Museum, located at the University of Manchester. Explore the extensive collection of natural history, archaeology, and anthropology exhibits. Admission is free, but donations are welcomed.
- Take a leisurely stroll through the vibrant Northern Quarter. Admire the street art, browse the independent boutiques and record stores, and stop for a coffee at one of the trendy cafes.

Evening:

- Indulge in a budget-friendly dinner at Rudy's Pizza, known for its delicious Neapolitan-style pizzas at affordable prices.
- End your day with some live music at a local venue like Band on the Wall or Soup Kitchen. Check their websites for upcoming gigs and ticket prices.

Day 2:

Morning:

- Start your day by exploring the fascinating Manchester Museum of Science and Industry. Discover the city's industrial heritage through interactive exhibits and demonstrations. Admission is free, but some special exhibitions may have an entrance fee.

Lunch:

- Enjoy a hearty lunch at the Corn Exchange, a historic building converted into a food hall with a variety of affordable dining options.

Afternoon:

- Take a guided tour of the iconic Old Trafford Stadium, home to Manchester United Football Club. Explore the museum, learn about the club's history, and walk through the players' tunnel. Ticket prices for the tour start at around £20.

Evening:

- Experience the vibrant nightlife in the lively area of the Printworks. Enjoy a meal at one of the budget-friendly restaurants, catch a movie at the cinema, or try your luck at the Bierkeller Entertainment Complex with its affordable drinks and live entertainment.

Day 3:

Morning:

- Explore the beautiful Heaton Park, one of the largest municipal parks in Europe. Take a leisurely walk through the park's expansive green spaces, visit the animal farm, and enjoy the scenic views. Admission to the park is free, but there may be charges for some attractions.

Lunch:

- Have a picnic in the park or enjoy a meal at the Heaton Park Café, offering a range of affordable options.

Afternoon:

- Visit the National Football Museum, located in the city center. Immerse yourself in the history of football through interactive exhibits and displays. Admission is free, but donations are encouraged.

Evening:

- Treat yourself to a budget-friendly dinner at the Curry Mile in Rusholme. Sample delicious and affordable South Asian cuisine from the many restaurants lining the street.

Total estimated expenses for three days:

- Accommodation (budget hotel or hostel): £150-£200
- Meals: £100-£150
- Transportation (public transport, taxis, etc.): £30-£50
- Attractions (optional tours, special exhibitions): £20-£40
- Miscellaneous (souvenirs, drinks, etc.): £50-£100

7 Days Manchester Travel Plan

Day 1:

Morning:

- Arrive in Manchester and check into your accommodation.

- Take a walking tour of the city center to familiarize yourself with the main landmarks and attractions.
- Visit the Manchester Cathedral and Chetham's Library, both offering free admission.

Lunch:

- Grab a quick and affordable lunch at the Arndale Market.

Afternoon:

- Explore the Manchester Museum, admission is free.
- Take a stroll through the Northern Quarter, known for its vibrant street art and independent shops.

Evening:

- Enjoy dinner at Rudy's Pizza.
- Catch a live music performance at a local venue like Band on the Wall.

Day 2:

Morning:

- Visit the Museum of Science and Industry, free admission.
- Explore the Castlefield area, home to Roman ruins and canals.

Lunch:

- Have a meal at the Corn Exchange.

Afternoon:

- Take a guided tour of Old Trafford Stadium (Manchester United Football Club) with ticket prices starting at around £20.

Evening:

- Experience the nightlife in the Printworks area.

Day 3:

Morning:

- Explore Heaton Park, free admission.
- Visit the National Football Museum, free admission.

Lunch:

- Enjoy a picnic in Heaton Park or have a meal at the park's café.

Afternoon:

- Explore the Manchester Art Gallery, free admission.
- Take a walk along the vibrant Oxford Road, known for its cultural institutions and lively atmosphere.

Evening:

- Have dinner in the Curry Mile area.

Day 4:

Morning:

- Take a day trip to the nearby city of Liverpool, known for its Beatles heritage and historic waterfront. Train tickets from Manchester to Liverpool start at around £10.

Lunch:

- Enjoy a meal at a local eatery in Liverpool.

Afternoon:

- Visit The Beatles Story museum and explore the Albert Dock area.

Evening:

- Return to Manchester and have dinner at a restaurant of your choice.

Day 5:

Morning:

- Visit the Whitworth Art Gallery, free admission.
- Explore the University of Manchester campus.

Lunch:

- Have a meal at a budget-friendly restaurant near the university.

Afternoon:

- Visit the John Rylands Library, free admission.
- Take a walk through the vibrant Chinatown area.

Evening:

- Enjoy dinner at a Chinese restaurant in Chinatown.

Day 6:

Morning:

- Take a day trip to the picturesque Peak District National Park, located just outside Manchester. Enjoy hiking, nature walks, and breathtaking scenery.

Lunch:

- Pack a picnic lunch to enjoy in the Peak District or have a meal at a local pub.

Afternoon:

- Continue exploring the Peak District, visit charming villages like Castleton or Bakewell.

Evening:
- Return to Manchester and have dinner at a restaurant of your choice.

Day 7:

Morning:

- Visit the People's History Museum, free admission.
- Explore the bohemian district of Didsbury, known for its cafes and independent shops.

Lunch:
- Enjoy a meal at a café or restaurant in Didsbury.

Afternoon:

- Visit the Trafford Centre, one of the UK's largest shopping centers.
- Explore the Lowry Outlet Mall and enjoy discounted shopping.

Evening:

- Have a farewell dinner at a restaurant of your choice.

Estimated expenses for seven days:

- Accommodation (budget hotel or hostel): £400-£600
- Meals: £300-£400
- Transportation (public transport, taxis, etc.): £60-£100
- Attractions (optional tours, special exhibitions): £50-£100
- Day trips (including train tickets): £30-£80

CHAPTER 4: PLANNING A TRIP TO MANCHESTER

What To Take For Your Trip

When preparing for your trip to Manchester, it's essential to pack wisely to ensure a comfortable and enjoyable experience. Here are some key items to consider taking with you:

1. **Weather-Appropriate Clothing:** Manchester has a temperate maritime climate, so be prepared for changing weather conditions. Pack a variety of clothing options, including lightweight layers, a waterproof jacket, and comfortable shoes for walking. Don't forget to bring an umbrella or a compact raincoat, as rain showers are common throughout the year.
2. **Travel Documents:** Ensure you have all the necessary travel documents, including your passport, identification cards, travel insurance information, and any printed reservations or tickets. It's also advisable to

have digital copies of these documents saved on your phone or other electronic devices.
3. **Adapters and Chargers:** Remember to pack the appropriate power adapters for your electronic devices, as the plug sockets in the UK use a different standard than in many other countries. Additionally, bring chargers for your phone, camera, or other devices to keep them powered throughout your trip.
4. **Money and Payment Options**: Carry some cash in the local currency, British pounds (GBP), for small purchases and emergencies. However, it's also recommended to have alternative payment options like credit or debit cards, as they are widely accepted in Manchester.
5. **Travel Guide or Maps:** Bring a travel guidebook or download a reliable travel app to help you navigate Manchester and discover the best attractions, dining options, and local tips. It's also beneficial to have a map of the city to assist you in getting around.
6. **Medications and First Aid:** If you take any prescription medications, ensure you have an adequate supply for the duration of your trip. It's also advisable to pack a small first aid kit with essential items like bandages,

pain relievers, and any personal medications or remedies you might need.
7. **Travel-sized Toiletries:** Pack travel-sized toiletries, including shampoo, conditioner, toothpaste, and soap. It's also worth including sunscreen, lip balm, and insect repellent, depending on the season and activities you plan to undertake.
8. **Portable Charger:** A portable charger can be incredibly useful, especially if you're relying heavily on your smartphone for navigation, communication, and capturing memories. It ensures that you won't run out of battery during your explorations.
9. **Entertainment:** For moments of downtime during your trip, bring a book, magazine, or your preferred form of entertainment to keep you occupied during flights, train journeys, or relaxing moments.
10. **Reusable Water Bottle:** Staying hydrated is essential, so pack a reusable water bottle to refill throughout the day. Manchester has plenty of water refill stations available, which helps reduce plastic waste and keeps you hydrated on the go.

Remember to check any specific requirements or restrictions regarding luggage size and weight set by your airline or transportation provider before packing. Additionally, consider the season and the specific activities you plan to engage in when finalizing your packing list. By being well-prepared, you can make the most of your trip to Manchester and ensure a smooth and enjoyable travel experience.

Night Spot In Manchester

Manchester is renowned for its vibrant nightlife, offering a diverse range of nightspots to suit every taste. Whether you're looking for a trendy club, a cozy pub, or a live music venue, Manchester has it all. Here are some popular nightspots in the city:

1. **The Northern Quarter:** Known for its bohemian atmosphere, the Northern Quarter is a hub of creativity and nightlife. It boasts a wide array of independent bars, pubs, and clubs. You can explore hidden gems like the quirky cocktail bar, Cain & Grain, or enjoy live music at Band on the Wall, a legendary music venue.
2. **Deansgate Locks:** Situated near the city center, Deansgate Locks is a bustling area lined with stylish bars and clubs. This vibrant spot offers a mix of entertainment, from sophisticated cocktail lounges to high-energy dance clubs. Popular venues include Revolution, The Milton Club, and Gorilla.
3. **The Warehouse Project:** For electronic music enthusiasts, The Warehouse Project is a must-visit. This world-renowned event series hosts a lineup of renowned DJs and artists in unique venues across Manchester. From underground techno to house music, The Warehouse Project guarantees an unforgettable night of dancing and music.
4. **Canal Street:** Located in Manchester's Gay Village, Canal Street is a lively and inclusive area known for its LGBTQ+ nightlife. It's home to numerous bars and clubs that cater to diverse crowds. The iconic Canal Street is

a vibrant and inclusive hub where everyone can enjoy a fantastic night out.

5. **Albert Hall:** Housed in a former Wesleyan chapel, Albert Hall is an awe-inspiring venue that hosts live music events and club nights. The stunning architecture combined with a fantastic sound system creates an unforgettable experience. From indie bands to electronic acts, Albert Hall offers a diverse range of performances.

6. **Chinatown:** Manchester's Chinatown comes alive at night, offering a variety of restaurants, karaoke bars, and late-night venues. You can savor delicious Chinese cuisine, enjoy karaoke with friends, or relax in a cozy tea house. The vibrant atmosphere makes Chinatown a popular spot for a night out.

Whether you're into live music, dancing, or simply enjoying a few drinks in a cozy pub, Manchester's nightspots have something for everyone. The city's diverse and vibrant nightlife scene ensures that you'll find the perfect spot to create unforgettable memories and enjoy the energetic atmosphere of this dynamic city.

Culture And People

Culture in Manchester is deeply influenced by its industrial past, as the city played a crucial role during the Industrial Revolution. This heritage is reflected in the stunning Victorian architecture that can be seen throughout the city, such as the iconic Manchester Town Hall and the industrial warehouses that have been repurposed into trendy venues.

Music has always been an integral part of Manchester's cultural identity. The city has produced numerous influential bands and artists, from The Smiths and Oasis to The Stone Roses and Joy Division. The legendary nightclub, The Haçienda, was at the forefront of the UK's rave and dance music scene in the 1980s and 1990s. Today, Manchester continues to be a thriving music hub with a vibrant live music scene and numerous music festivals and events throughout the year.

Manchester is also known for its thriving arts and cultural institutions. The city is home to world-class museums, including the Manchester Art Gallery and the Whitworth Art Gallery, showcasing an impressive collection of art spanning different periods and genres. The Royal Exchange Theatre and the Bridgewater Hall are renowned venues for theater and classical music performances.

The people of Manchester are known for their warmth, resilience, and community spirit. Mancunians have a strong sense of identity and pride in their city. They are known for their friendliness and are often described as down-to-earth and approachable. The city's diverse population contributes to its multicultural fabric, with various communities living side by side and adding to the city's cultural tapestry.

Mancunians are also passionate about their sports, particularly football. Manchester is home to two major football clubs, Manchester United and Manchester City, and the city comes alive on match days with a sea of fans donning their team colors.

CHAPTER 5

Top 10 Best Local Cuisine In Manchester

1. **Manchester Tart:** This traditional dessert is a must-try when in the city. It consists of a shortcrust pastry tart filled with a layer of raspberry jam, a creamy custard filling, and topped with coconut flakes. It's a delicious and indulgent treat that showcases Manchester's culinary heritage.

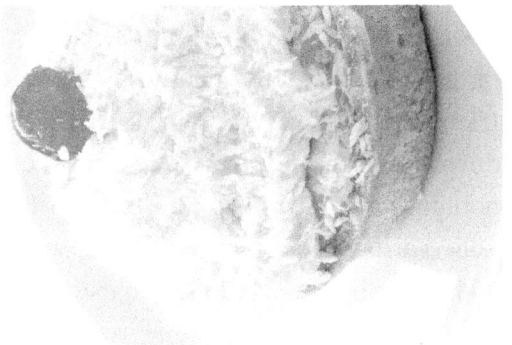

2. **Bury Black Pudding:** A staple of English cuisine, Bury Black Pudding is a type of blood sausage made with pork fat, oatmeal, and blood. It has a rich and savory flavor, often enjoyed as part of a full English breakfast or in a black pudding and apple salad.

3. **Beef and Ale Pie:** A classic British comfort food, the beef and ale pie is a hearty dish filled with tender chunks of beef cooked in rich gravy and encased in a buttery pastry. It's a satisfying and flavorful dish that epitomizes British pub fare.

4. **Lancashire Hotpot:** Originating from the nearby county of Lancashire, this dish is a meat and potato casserole that is slow-cooked to perfection. Traditionally

made with lamb or mutton, it features layers of meat, onions, and potatoes, all cooked together until tender and flavorful.

5. **Fish and Chips:** No visit to the UK is complete without indulging in the beloved fish and chips. Crispy battered fish, typically cod or haddock, served with chunky fries, mushy peas, and tartar sauce, is a quintessential British dish that can be found in numerous fish and chip shops across Manchester.

6. **Butter Pie:** A lesser-known local specialty, the butter pie is a savory pie filled with a mixture of mashed potatoes, onions, and butter. It's a simple yet satisfying dish that has a creamy and comforting flavor.

7. **Manchester Egg:** A twist on the classic Scotch egg, the Manchester egg features a pickled egg wrapped in black pudding and coated with breadcrumbs. It's a unique and

flavorsome snack that showcases the city's creativity in reinventing traditional dishes.

8. **Eccles Cake:** Originally from the nearby town of Eccles, this sweet pastry is made with flaky pastry filled with a mixture of currants, sugar, and spices. It's often enjoyed with a cup of tea or coffee as a delightful afternoon treat.

9. **Curry Mile Cuisine:** Located on Wilmslow Road, the Curry Mile is renowned for its

wide array of Indian and Pakistani restaurants. From fragrant biryanis and spicy curries to delicious kebabs and naan bread, this vibrant stretch offers an authentic taste of South Asian cuisine.

10. **Craft Beers and Ales:** While not a cuisine per se, Manchester has a thriving craft beer scene. Numerous breweries and pubs in the city produce and serve a wide variety of locally brewed beers and ales, offering a taste of Manchester's vibrant brewing culture.

Money Matters And Saving Tips

Money matters and saving tips are important considerations when visiting Manchester. Here are some strategies to help you manage your finances effectively and make the most of your budget:

1. **Currency Exchange:** Before your trip, research the best options for currency exchange to ensure you get the most favorable rates. Compare rates from banks, exchange offices, or use reputable online services to exchange your money.
2. **Budgeting**: Plan a realistic budget for your trip, considering accommodation, transportation, meals, attractions, and other expenses. Stick to your budget and track your spending to avoid overspending.
3. **Public Transportation**: Utilize Manchester's efficient public transportation system, including buses and trams, which offer affordable fares and convenient routes. Consider purchasing a travel pass or card for unlimited travel during your stay.
4. **Eating Out:** Manchester offers a range of dining options to suit different budgets. To save money, consider eating at local pubs, cafes, or street food stalls. Look out for lunch specials or early bird menus that offer discounted prices.
5. **Grocery Shopping**: If your accommodation allows, consider preparing some of your meals using groceries from local supermarkets. This can be a cost-effective option for breakfast or lunch and also

provides an opportunity to sample local produce.

6. **Free Attractions and Activities:** Manchester has several free attractions and activities to enjoy, such as museums, art galleries, parks, and historical sites. Take advantage of these offerings to enrich your experience without spending money on entrance fees.
7. **Discounted Tickets:** Look out for discounted tickets or special offers for attractions, shows, or events. Check websites, social media pages, or tourist information centers for any ongoing promotions or discounts.
8. **Water:** Instead of purchasing bottled water, carry a reusable water bottle and refill it at public water fountains or ask for tap water at restaurants, as it is safe and free.
9. **Student Discounts:** If you're a student, make sure to carry your student ID card. Many attractions, restaurants, and shops offer discounted prices for students, so take advantage of these savings.
10. **Cash vs. Card:** While most places in Manchester accept card payments, it's always a good idea to carry some cash for small purchases or places that may not accept cards.

Remember to keep your belongings secure and be cautious with your spending while exploring the city. By implementing these money-saving tips, you can make the most of your budget and have a rewarding experience in Manchester without breaking the bank.

Local Customs And Etiquette

When visiting Manchester, it's helpful to familiarize yourself with the local customs and etiquette to ensure a smooth and respectful experience. Here are some key customs and etiquette practices to keep in mind:

1. **Greetings:** Mancunians are generally friendly and approachable. When meeting someone for the first time, a firm handshake

and a friendly smile are appropriate. It's common to use "please" and "thank you" when interacting with locals.
2. **Queuing:** Queueing is taken seriously in Manchester. Whether it's waiting for public transportation, ordering food, or entering a venue, it's important to respect the queue and wait patiently for your turn.
3. **Personal Space:** While Mancunians are generally friendly, they also value personal space. It's important to maintain an appropriate physical distance when engaging in conversations or in crowded areas.
4. **Punctuality:** Being punctual is highly valued in Manchester. If you have scheduled appointments or plans, it's best to arrive on time. If you anticipate being late, it's considerate to inform the other party in advance.
5. **Tipping:** Tipping is customary in restaurants, cafes, and bars. As a general guideline, leaving a 10-15% tip for good service is appreciated. Some establishments may include a service charge, so it's advisable to check the bill before adding an additional tip.
6. **Cultural Sensitivity:** Manchester is a diverse city, and it's important to be respectful of different cultures and customs.

Avoid making derogatory comments or engaging in behavior that may be offensive to others.

7. **Smoking:** Manchester has strict laws regarding smoking in public places. Smoking is prohibited in most indoor areas, including restaurants, pubs, and public transportation. It's important to adhere to these regulations and only smoke in designated smoking areas.
8. **Dress Code:** Manchester has a relaxed and casual dress code in most settings. However, some upscale restaurants, theaters, or events may have specific dress requirements. It's advisable to check in advance to ensure you are appropriately dressed.
9. **Photography:** When taking photographs of people or private property, it's polite to ask for permission first. Some places may have restrictions on photography, so it's important to respect any signage or guidelines provided.
10. **Football Culture:** Manchester is known for its passionate football culture. If attending a football match, respect the traditions and customs of the game. Avoid engaging in offensive chants or displaying disrespectful behavior towards opposing teams or fans.

By being mindful of these local customs and etiquette practices, you can show respect for the local culture, interact positively with the people of Manchester, and have a memorable and enjoyable experience in the city.

Tipping In Manchester

Tipping is a customary practice in Manchester, and it is generally expected to leave a tip for good service. While tipping is not mandatory, it is appreciated and considered a gesture of gratitude towards service staff. Here are some guidelines to keep in mind when it comes to tipping in Manchester:

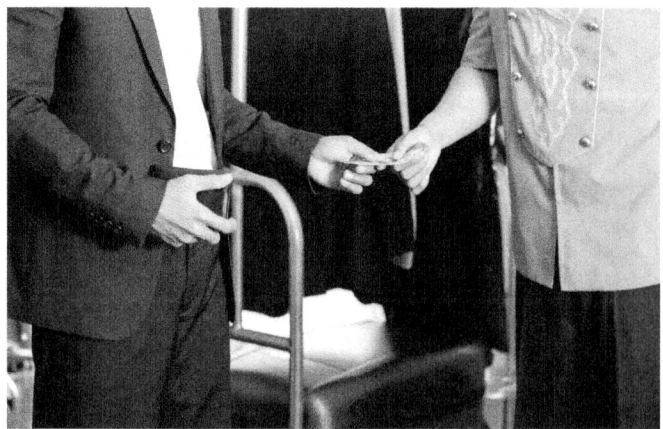

1. **Restaurants and Cafes:** In restaurants and cafes, it is customary to leave a tip of around

10-15% of the total bill for good service. Some establishments may include a service charge on the bill, in which case, an additional tip is not necessary. However, if no service charge is included, leaving a tip is appreciated.
2. **Bars and Pubs:** In bars and pubs, it is common to leave a small tip of a few coins when ordering drinks. While it is not necessary to tip for every round, leaving a tip at the end of the evening is a polite gesture.
3. **Taxis:** When using a taxi service, it is customary to round up the fare to the nearest pound or leave a small tip, especially if the driver has provided good service or assisted with luggage.
4. **Other Services:** In other service industries such as hair salons, spas, or hotels, tipping is appreciated but not always expected. It is customary to tip around 10% of the service cost for good service.

It's worth noting that some establishments may include a discretionary service charge on the bill. In such cases, it is up to the individual whether to leave an additional tip. Additionally, always check the bill to ensure that a service charge has not already been added before adding an extra tip.

Ultimately, tipping in Manchester is a personal choice, and the amount you choose to tip may vary based on your satisfaction with the service provided. It's important to consider the quality of service and your own budget when deciding on the appropriate amount to tip.

CHAPTER 6: TIPS AND CONSIDERATION ENTRY REQUIREMENT

Safety And Preparedness

Safety and preparedness are important considerations for any traveler visiting Manchester. While the city is generally safe, it's always wise to take precautions to ensure a secure and enjoyable experience. Here are some tips to help you stay safe and prepared during your time in Manchester:

1. **Stay Aware of Your Surroundings:** Be vigilant and aware of your surroundings at all times, especially in crowded places, tourist attractions, and public transportation hubs. Avoid displaying valuable items and keep your belongings secure.
2. **Use Reliable Transportation:** When using public transportation or taxis, choose licensed and reputable providers. If you're unsure, ask for recommendations from locals or your accommodation staff

3. **Secure Your Accommodation:** Choose accommodation in safe and well-populated areas. Ensure your lodging has proper security measures, such as lockable doors and windows, and use the in-room safe for storing valuables.
4. **Emergency Contacts:** Save important contact numbers, including the local police, ambulance, and your embassy or consulate, in your phone or on a printed list. In case of any emergencies, you can quickly access the necessary help and assistance.
5. **Travel Insurance:** It is strongly recommended to have comprehensive travel insurance that covers medical emergencies, trip cancellations, and lost or stolen belongings. Familiarize yourself with the terms and coverage of your insurance policy before your trip.
6. **Health and Medications:** If you have any pre-existing medical conditions or require specific medications, ensure you have an ample supply for the duration of your stay. It's also advisable to carry a copy of your prescriptions or medical documents.
7. **Emergency Evacuation Plan:** Familiarize yourself with the emergency evacuation procedures of your accommodation, including fire exits and assembly points.

Take note of any safety instructions provided by your accommodation staff.
8. **Weather Precautions:** Manchester experiences variable weather conditions, so be prepared for rain, wind, or sudden temperature changes. Pack appropriate clothing and footwear for different weather scenarios to ensure your comfort and well-being.
9. **Digital Safety:** Use secure Wi-Fi networks and avoid accessing sensitive information or making financial transactions on public networks. Install security software on your electronic devices and regularly update them to protect against cyber threats.
10. **Local Laws and Customs:** Familiarize yourself with the local laws and customs of Manchester to avoid any inadvertent violations or misunderstandings. Respect the cultural norms and be mindful of any specific rules or regulations in certain areas or venues.

What To Do And What To Avoid When Visiting manchester

When visiting Manchester, there are plenty of things to do and see that will make your trip memorable. However, it's also important to be aware of certain aspects to avoid any potential issues. Here are some recommendations on what to do and what to avoid when visiting Manchester:

What to Do:

1. **Explore the City Centre:** Take a stroll through Manchester's city centre to discover its vibrant atmosphere, stunning architecture, and notable landmarks like Manchester Town Hall, the Manchester Cathedral, and the Royal Exchange Theatre.
2. **Visit Museums and Galleries:** Manchester is home to numerous museums and galleries, including the Manchester Museum, the Museum of Science and Industry, and the Manchester Art Gallery. Immerse yourself in art, history, and culture during your visit.

3. **Enjoy the Music Scene:** Manchester has a rich musical heritage, known for its influential bands like Oasis and The Smiths. Experience the city's live music scene by attending concerts or visiting iconic music venues such as the O2 Apollo Manchester or the Manchester Arena.
4. **Explore Football Culture:** Manchester is passionate about football, and a visit to the city wouldn't be complete without immersing yourself in its football culture. Take a stadium tour of Old Trafford, home of Manchester United, or visit the National Football Museum to learn more about the sport's history.
5. **Experience the Nightlife:** Manchester boasts a vibrant nightlife scene with a range of bars, clubs, and live music venues. From trendy cocktail bars to underground music clubs, there's something for everyone to enjoy.

What to Avoid:

1. **Petty Crime:** While Manchester is generally a safe city, it's important to remain vigilant and take precautions against petty crime. Avoid displaying valuable items

openly and be cautious of your surroundings, particularly in crowded areas.
2. **Unauthorized Street Traders:** Be cautious of unauthorized street traders selling counterfeit goods or engaging in scams. It's advisable to shop at legitimate stores and markets to ensure the quality and authenticity of your purchases.
3. **Late-Night Walking in Isolated Areas:** While Manchester is generally safe, it's wise to avoid walking alone in isolated or poorly lit areas, especially late at night. Stick to well-populated and well-lit areas, and consider using public transportation or taxis when necessary.
4. **Overindulging in Alcohol:** Manchester has a vibrant nightlife scene, but it's important to drink responsibly and know your limits. Excessive alcohol consumption can increase vulnerability and put you at risk.
5. **Engaging in Anti-Social Behavior:** Respect the local community and adhere to local laws and customs. Avoid engaging in anti-social behavior, excessive noise, or public disturbances that could disrupt the peace and well-being of the city and its residents.

By following these recommendations on what to do and what to avoid, you can have a rewarding and enjoyable experience during your visit to Manchester. Remember to stay informed, respect the local culture, and take necessary precautions to ensure a memorable trip.

CHAPTER 7: UNDERSTANDING INTERNATIONAL TRANSACTION FEES

Avoid Cell Phone Roaming Charges

If you're visiting Manchester and want to avoid expensive cell phone roaming charges, there are several strategies you can employ to stay connected without breaking the bank. Here are some tips to help you avoid cell phone roaming charges:

1. **Check with Your Provider:** Before your trip, contact your mobile service provider to inquire about their international roaming plans and rates. They may have specific packages or options available that can help you reduce roaming charges.
2. **Use Wi-Fi Whenever Possible:** Take advantage of free Wi-Fi hotspots available in hotels, cafes, restaurants, and public areas. Connect to Wi-Fi networks to make

calls, send messages, and use data-based apps without incurring roaming charges.
3. **Use Messaging Apps:** Instead of relying on traditional SMS texting, use messaging apps such as WhatsApp, Facebook Messenger, or iMessage (for iPhone users) to communicate with friends and family. These apps use internet data rather than cellular networks, allowing you to avoid SMS charges.
4. **Make Internet Calls:** Use internet-based calling services such as Skype, FaceTime, or Google Hangouts to make voice and video calls over Wi-Fi. These services often offer free or low-cost calls to other users and significantly reduce roaming charges.
5. **Buy a Local SIM Card:** Consider purchasing a local SIM card upon arrival in Manchester. This allows you to have a local phone number and access to local calling and data rates. Make sure your phone is unlocked and compatible with the local network before buying a SIM card.
6. **Enable Airplane Mode:** If you don't need to use your cellular data or make calls, switch your phone to airplane mode. This disables cellular connections and prevents any unintentional data usage or roaming charges. You can still connect to Wi-Fi networks while in airplane mode.

7. **Download Maps and Essential Information:** Before you arrive in Manchester, download offline maps and any essential information you may need during your trip. This ensures that you can access directions, points of interest, and other crucial details without relying on a cellular connection.
8. **Disable Automatic Updates and Background Data:** To minimize data usage, disable automatic app updates and restrict background data usage for non-essential apps. This prevents your phone from consuming data in the background, reducing the risk of unexpected charges.
9. **Consider Portable Wi-Fi Devices:** If you require constant internet access, consider renting or purchasing a portable Wi-Fi device, also known as a pocket Wi-Fi or Mi-Fi. These devices provide a secure Wi-Fi connection for your phone and other devices, allowing you to stay connected without relying on roaming.

Consider A Manchester Sim Card Or Mifi Device

When visiting Manchester, one option to consider for staying connected without incurring high roaming charges is using a Cork SIM card or a MiFi device.

Cork SIM cards are prepaid SIM cards that offer affordable local rates for calling, texting, and data usage. By purchasing a Cork SIM card upon arrival in Manchester, you can enjoy local calling and data plans, which are often more cost-effective than international roaming charges. Make sure your phone is unlocked and compatible with the network used by the Cork SIM card before making a purchase.

Alternatively, a MiFi device, also known as a portable Wi-Fi hotspot, can be a convenient option. These devices allow you to create your own Wi-Fi network by connecting to a local cellular network. You can connect multiple devices, such as smartphones, tablets, or laptops, to the MiFi device, enabling internet access for all your devices while on the go. MiFi devices are available for rent or purchase, and they often come with various data plans to suit your needs.

Both Cork SIM cards and MiFi devices provide flexibility and control over your connectivity options while in Manchester. They allow you to access the internet, make calls, and send messages using local rates, helping you avoid costly roaming charges. Before making a decision, compare the costs, coverage, and data allowances of different providers to find the best option for your needs.

Download Offline Map

When visiting Manchester, it's a good idea to download offline maps to your smartphone or tablet before you arrive. Having offline maps readily available can be incredibly helpful, especially if you don't have access to a reliable internet connection or want to avoid excessive data usage. Here are a few reasons why downloading offline maps for Manchester is beneficial:

1. **Access Without Data Connection:** With offline maps, you can navigate the streets, find attractions, and plan routes without relying on an active data connection. This is particularly useful if you're in areas with weak or no internet coverage or if you want to conserve your data for other purposes.
2. **Save Data and Roaming Charges:** By using offline maps, you can minimize data usage and avoid incurring roaming charges. Since the maps are stored locally on your device, you don't need to rely on a constant internet connection to access them.
3. **Reliable Navigation:** Offline maps provide reliable navigation even when GPS signals are weak. You can rely on the downloaded maps to guide you accurately to your

destination without interruptions caused by fluctuating signals.

4. **Quick Reference:** Offline maps allow you to quickly reference your location or find nearby points of interest, even when you're offline. This can be helpful for locating restaurants, attractions, public transportation, or any other places you want to visit in Manchester.

To download offline maps, you can use various map applications such as Google Maps, HERE WeGo, or MAPS.ME. These apps allow you to select a specific area and download it to your device for offline use. Remember to download the maps before your trip while you still have an internet connection, so you have them readily available when needed.

By having offline maps on hand, you can navigate Manchester with ease, save on data costs, and ensure you don't get lost even without an active internet connection. It's a simple and practical step to enhance your travel experience in the city.

Learn Basic Language

Learning a few basic phrases in the local language when visiting Manchester can greatly enhance your travel experience and help you communicate more effectively with locals. While English is widely spoken in Manchester, making an effort to learn some common greetings and expressions can show respect and foster positive interactions. Here are a few reasons why learning basic language skills can be beneficial:

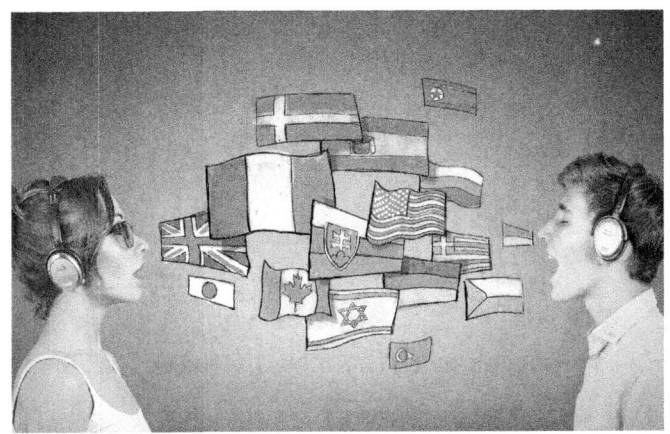

1. **Connect with Locals:** Speaking a few words in the local language can create a sense of connection and goodwill with the people you encounter in Manchester. Locals appreciate the effort and may be more open and receptive to engaging with you.
2. **Navigate Everyday Situations:** Learning basic phrases like greetings, please, thank you, and excuse me can be incredibly useful in everyday situations, such as ordering food, asking for directions, or making

purchases. It helps bridge the language barrier and makes communication smoother.
3. **Cultural Understanding:** Learning basic language skills also provides insights into the local culture. Language is closely tied to customs, traditions, and social norms. By understanding a few phrases, you can gain a deeper appreciation for the local culture and show respect for their way of life.
4. **Enhance Travel Experience:** Knowing basic language skills can enhance your overall travel experience. It allows you to interact with locals, seek recommendations, and immerse yourself more fully in the local environment. You may also discover hidden gems or unique experiences that are off the beaten path.

To get started, familiarize yourself with simple greetings like "hello," "goodbye," and "thank you." Learn basic phrases for ordering food, asking for directions, and making polite requests. You can find language learning resources online, use language learning apps, or even take a short introductory language course. Practice with locals whenever you have the opportunity and don't be afraid to make mistakes – locals will appreciate your efforts and may even help you improve.

Remember, the goal is not to become fluent but to show a genuine interest in the local language and culture. Even a few basic phrases can go a long way in making your time in Manchester more enjoyable and rewarding.

Cash At The Airport Is Expensive

When traveling to Manchester, it's important to be aware that obtaining cash at the airport can be expensive. Airports typically have higher exchange rates and additional fees compared to other currency exchange options. Here are a few reasons why cash at the airport in Manchester can be costly:

1. **Higher Exchange Rates:** Airport currency exchange services often offer less favorable exchange rates compared to banks, local

exchange offices, or ATMs located outside the airport. The rates at airports are typically adjusted to include a higher margin for the convenience of immediate access to cash.
2. **Commission and Fees:** Currency exchange services at airports may charge additional commission or service fees on top of the already inflated exchange rates. These fees can significantly reduce the amount of currency you receive in exchange for your money.
3. **Limited Options:** Airports usually have a limited number of currency exchange providers, which reduces competition and gives them more control over the rates they offer. This lack of competition can result in less competitive rates and higher costs for travelers.
4. **Convenience Premium:** The convenience of exchanging money at the airport comes with a price. Airport currency exchange services cater to the immediate needs of travelers who require cash upon arrival, and they charge a premium for the convenience factor.

To avoid the higher costs associated with obtaining cash at the airport in Manchester, consider the following alternatives:

5. **Pre-order Currency:** If you prefer to have cash on hand when you arrive, consider pre-ordering your currency from a reputable online exchange service or your local bank. This allows you to secure more competitive rates and avoid the extra fees charged at airport exchanges.
6. **Use ATMs:** ATMs located outside the airport, in the city center, or near your accommodation, often offer better exchange rates and lower fees compared to airport exchanges. Use your debit or credit card to withdraw cash in the local currency. However, be mindful of any fees charged by your bank for international withdrawals.
7. **Credit and Debit Cards:** Many establishments in Manchester, including hotels, restaurants, and shops, accept credit and debit cards. Using your card for purchases can be a convenient and cost-effective option, as it often provides a more favorable exchange rate and may have lower fees compared to exchanging cash.
8. **Digital Payment Methods:** Manchester is a modern city with a wide acceptance of digital payment methods such as contactless cards and mobile payment apps. Consider utilizing these options for smaller

transactions to avoid the need for excessive cash.

CONCLUSION

Tips for solo travelers, families and LGBTQ + travelers

Manchester is a vibrant and diverse city that welcomes solo travelers, families, and LGBTQ+ travelers with open arms. Here are some tips to enhance the experience for each group:

For Solo Travelers:

1. **Safety Awareness:** Like any city, it's important to stay aware of your surroundings and take basic safety precautions. Stick to well-lit and populated areas, especially at night, and trust your instincts.
2. **Join Group Activities:** Engage in group activities such as walking tours, pub crawls, or local meetups. This is a great way to meet fellow travelers and make new friends while exploring the city.
3. **Utilize Public Transportation:** Manchester has an extensive public transportation network. Use buses, trams, and trains to navigate the city easily and efficiently.

Consider getting a transport pass to save money on multiple journeys.

For Families:

1. **Visit Family-Friendly Attractions:** Manchester offers various family-friendly attractions such as the Museum of Science and Industry, LEGOLAND Discovery Centre, and the Manchester Museum. Plan visits to these places to keep children entertained and engaged.
2. **Parks and Green Spaces:** Manchester boasts beautiful parks and green spaces where families can enjoy picnics, walks, and outdoor activities. Heaton Park, Fletcher Moss Botanical Garden, and Platt Fields Park are just a few examples.
3. **Family-Oriented Accommodations:** Look for family-oriented accommodations that offer amenities like family rooms, child-friendly facilities, and play areas. Many hotels in Manchester cater to families and provide a comfortable stay for parents and children.

For LGBTQ+ Travelers:

1. **LGBTQ+ Scene:** Manchester has a vibrant LGBTQ+ scene, particularly in the Gay Village. Explore the area's bars, clubs, and events for a lively and inclusive atmosphere.
2. **LGBTQ+ Friendly Accommodations:** Choose accommodations that are LGBTQ+ friendly and located near LGBTQ+ hotspots. Many hotels in Manchester actively welcome LGBTQ+ travelers and provide a safe and inclusive environment.
3. **Pride Events:** Manchester hosts one of the largest Pride events in the UK, attracting visitors from around the world. Check the dates of Pride celebrations and plan your trip accordingly to immerse yourself in the vibrant festivities.
4. **LGBTQ+ Support Services:** Familiarize yourself with LGBTQ+ support services and organizations in Manchester. They can provide information, resources, and assistance if needed during your visit.

Additional Resources And Contact Information

1. **Tourist Information Centers:** The Visit Manchester Visitor Information Centre is located in Piccadilly Gardens and provides a wealth of information on attractions, events,

maps, and local services. They can offer recommendations, book tours, and provide assistance to enhance your visit. Contact information: Visit Manchester Visitor Information Centre, 1 Piccadilly Gardens, Manchester M1 1RG, Phone: +44 871 222 8223.

2. **Emergency Services:** In case of emergencies, dial 999 for immediate assistance from the police, fire department, or ambulance services. For non-emergency police assistance, dial 101. It's important to have these numbers handy for any unforeseen situations.
3. **Medical Services:** If you require medical assistance, Manchester has several hospitals and clinics. Manchester Royal Infirmary, located on Oxford Road, is a major hospital in the city. For non-emergency medical advice, you can contact the NHS 111 helpline.
4. **Transportation Contacts:** For public transportation information, including buses, trams, and trains, contact Transport for Greater Manchester (TfGM). They can provide route information, schedules, and help you plan your journeys. TfGM Customer Services can be reached at 0161 244 1000.

5. **Embassy and Consulate Information:** If you're a foreign visitor and require assistance from your country's embassy or consulate, it's essential to have their contact information readily available. Contact your embassy or consulate in the UK to know their location and emergency contact details.
6. **Local Event Listings:** Stay up to date with the latest events, concerts, and performances happening in Manchester. Websites such as Visit Manchester (www.visitmanchester.com) and local newspapers like Manchester Evening News provide comprehensive event listings.
7. **Online Travel Forums:** Utilize online travel forums and communities to connect with fellow travelers and locals who can offer valuable insights, recommendations, and tips for your visit to Manchester. Websites like TripAdvisor and Lonely Planet's Thorn Tree forum are popular platforms for exchanging travel information.

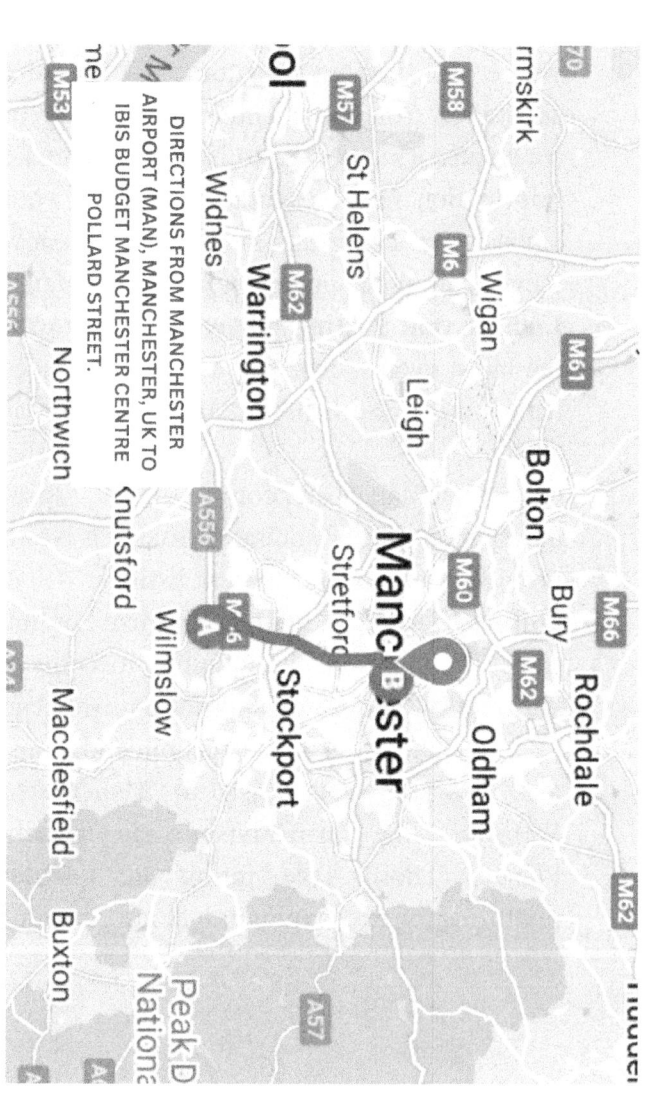

DIRECTIONS FROM MANCHESTER AIRPORT (MAN), MANCHESTER, UK TO IBIS BUDGET MANCHESTER CENTRE POLLARD STREET.

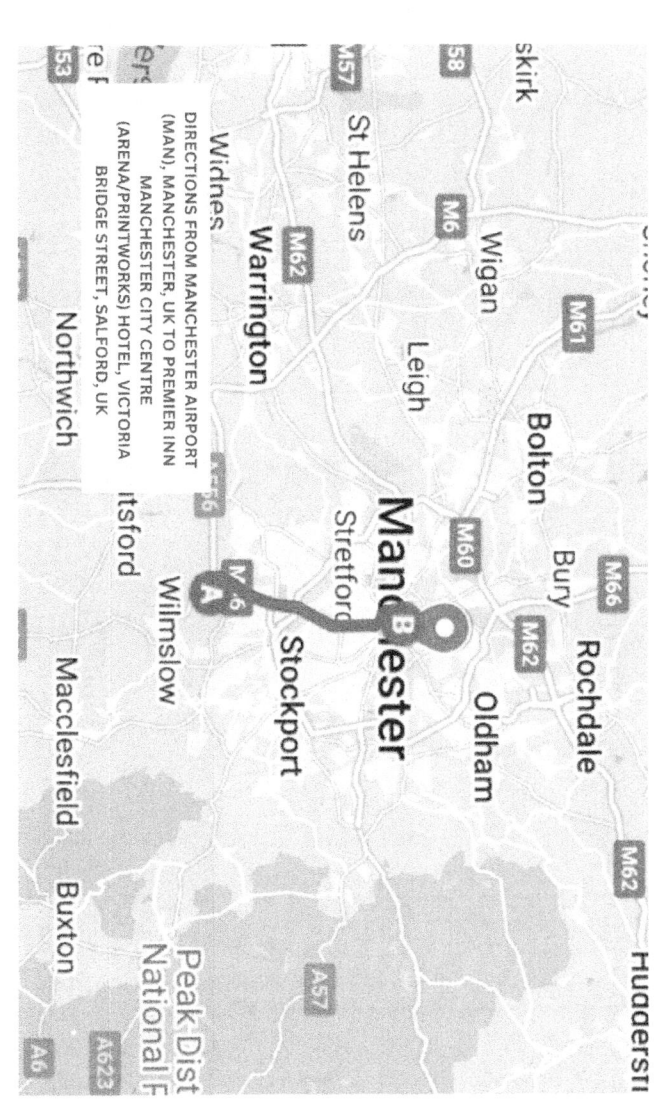

DIRECTIONS FROM MANCHESTER AIRPORT (MAN), MANCHESTER, UK TO PREMIER INN MANCHESTER CITY CENTRE (ARENA/PRINTWORKS) HOTEL, VICTORIA BRIDGE STREET, SALFORD, UK

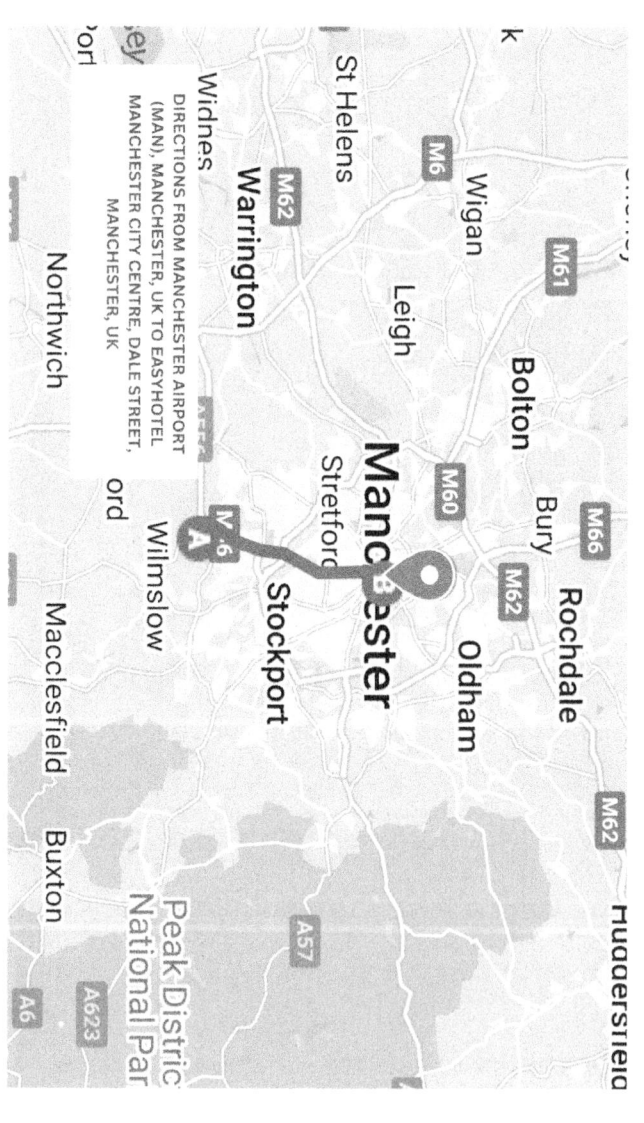

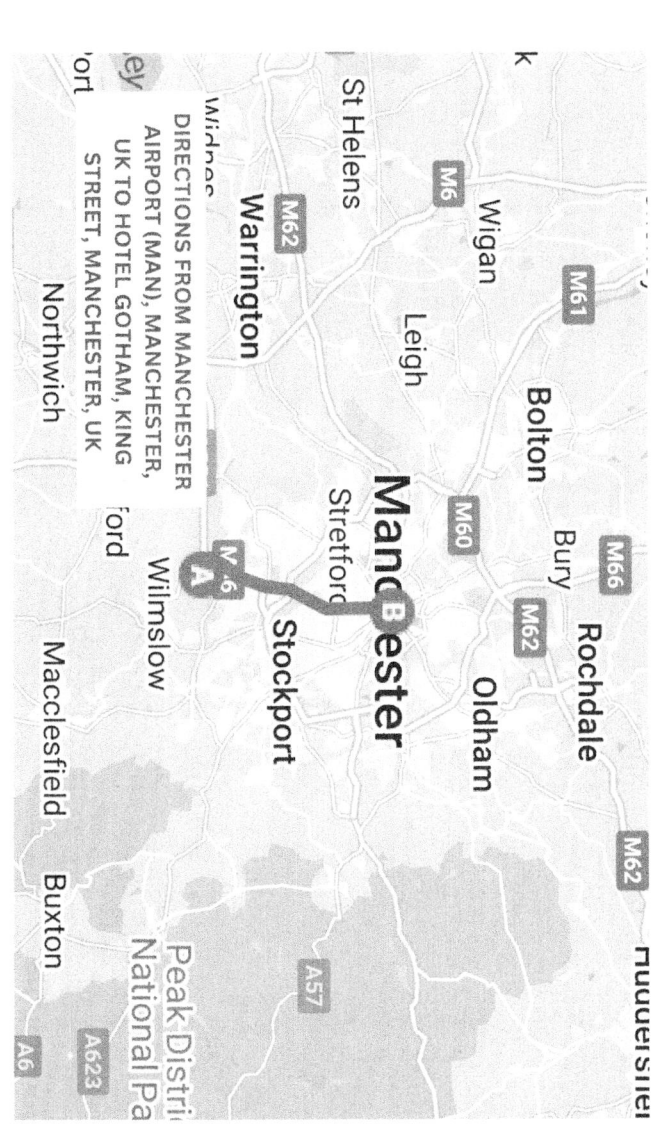

DIRECTIONS FROM MANCHESTER AIRPORT (MAN), MANCHESTER, UK TO HOTEL GOTHAM, KING STREET, MANCHESTER, UK

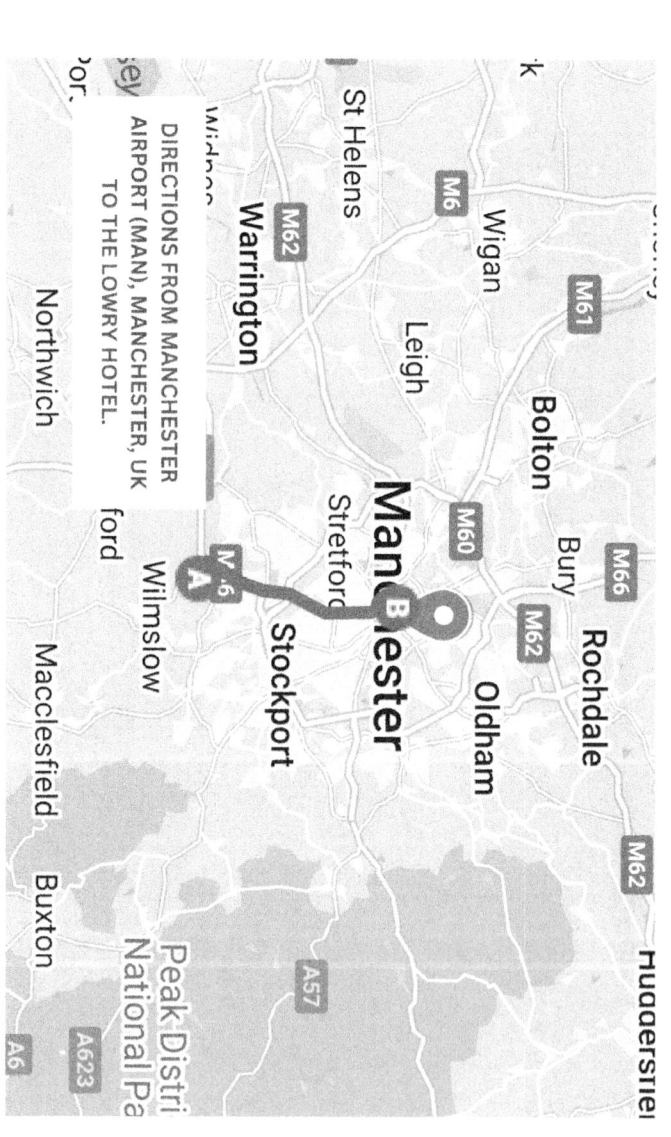

DIRECTIONS FROM MANCHESTER AIRPORT (MAN), MANCHESTER, UK TO THE LOWRY HOTEL.

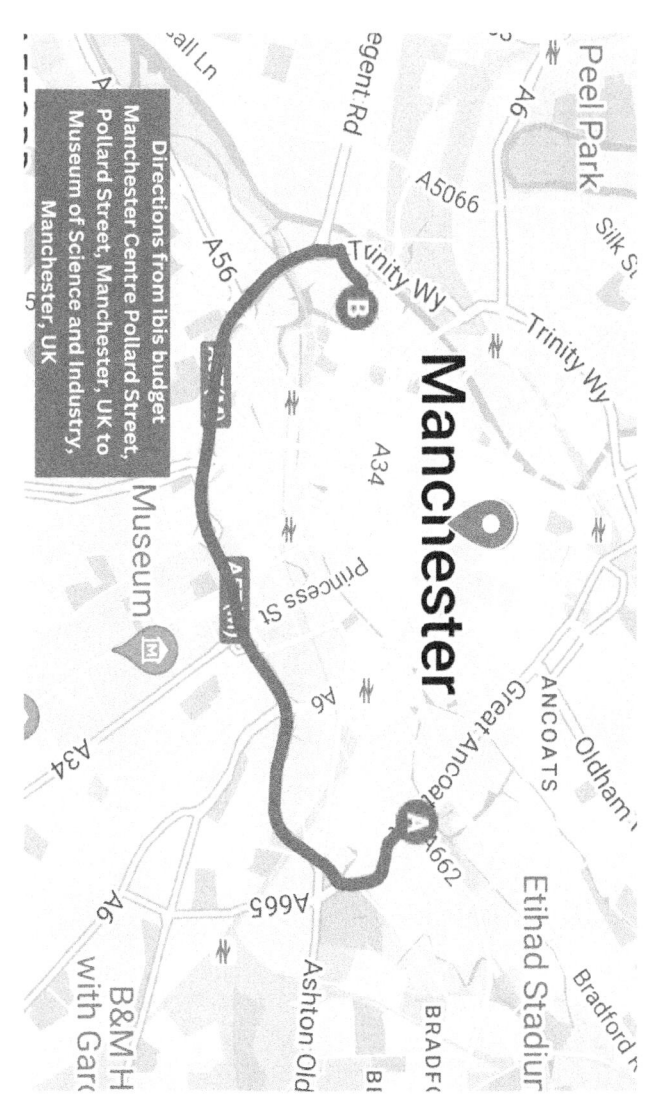

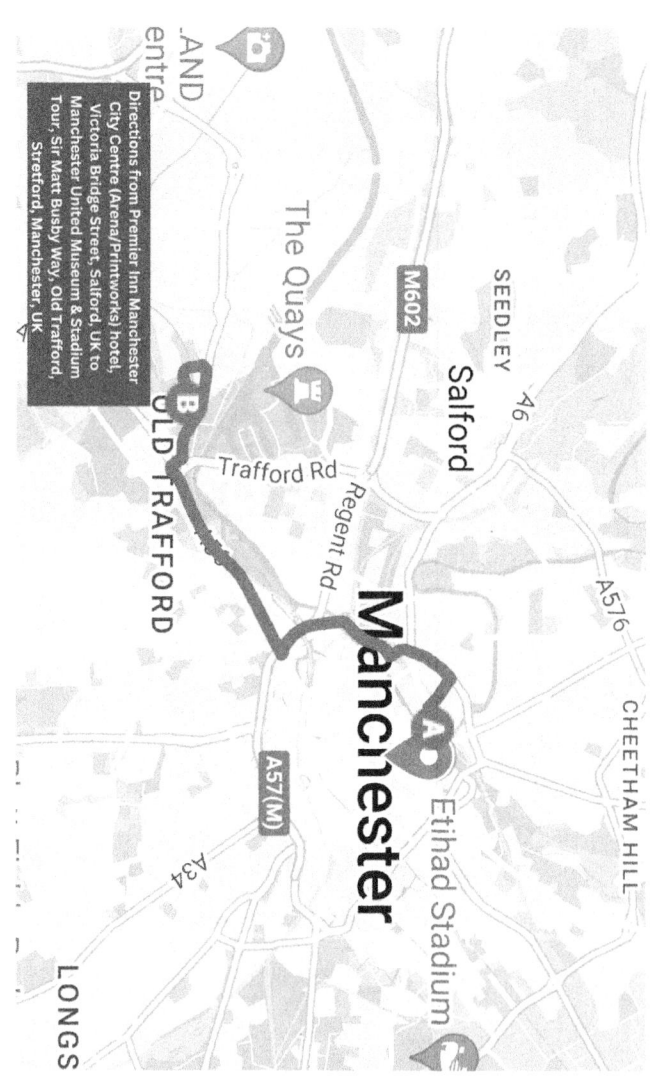

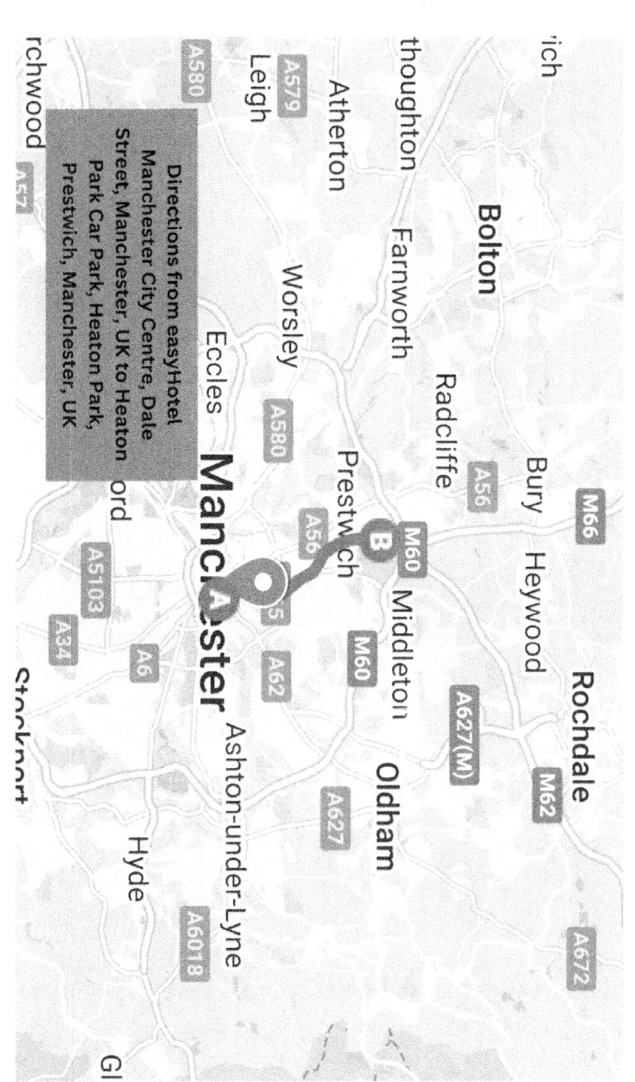

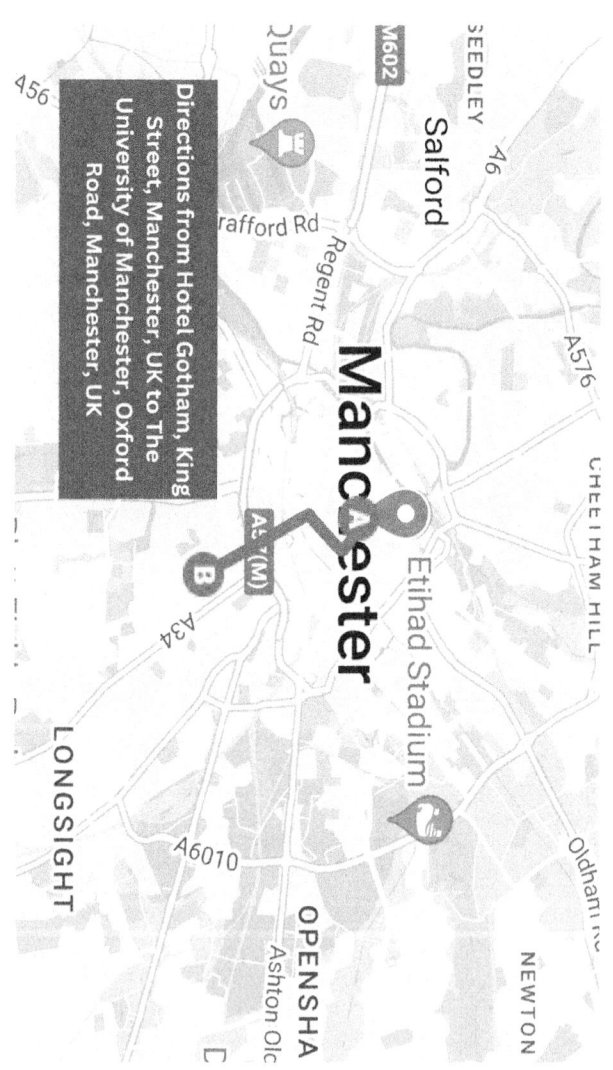

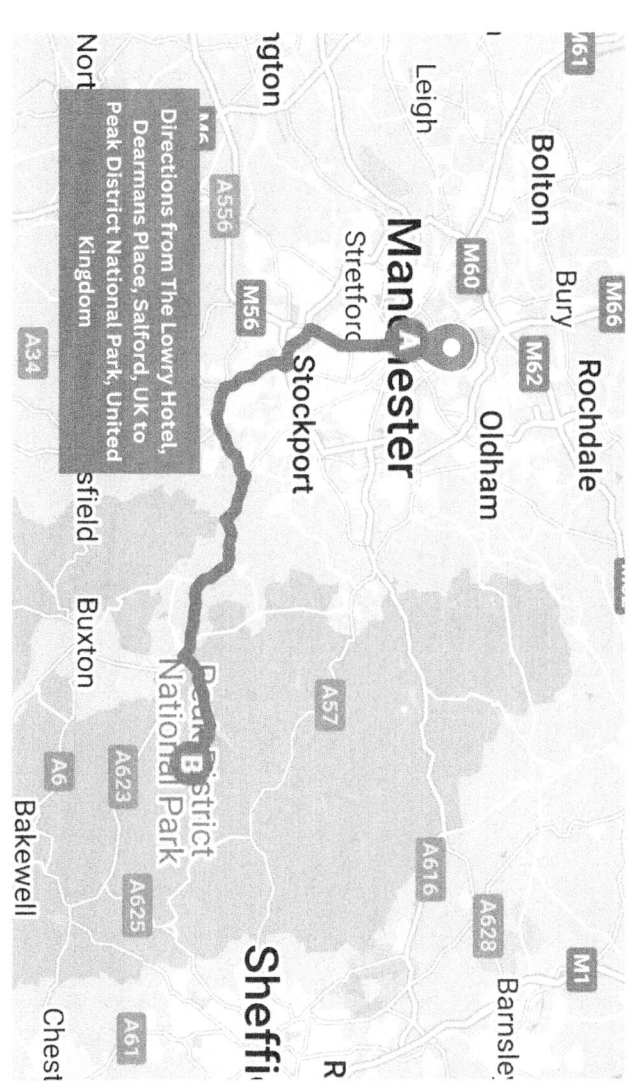

Printed in Great Britain
by Amazon

34548823R00061